THANKSGIVING CHUCKLES & CHOW

Anna Anderhagen

Consulting Editor, Diane Craig, MA/Reading Specialist

Super Sandcastle

An Imprint of Abdo Publishing
abdobooks.com

abdobooks.com

Published by Abdo Publishing, a division of ABDO, PO Box 398166, Minneapolis, Minnesota 55439.

Printed in the United States of America, North Mankato, Minnesota
102024
012025

THIS BOOK CONTAINS RECYCLED MATERIALS

Design: Layne Halvorsen, Mighty Media, Inc.
Production: Mighty Media, Inc.
Editor: Liz Salzmann
Cover Photographs: Mighty Media, Inc. (recipe photos); Shutterstock Images
Interior Photographs: Adobe Stock, 4 (leaves), 7 (child), 10 (frosting), 11 (frosting, crumbs), 12 (hands), 13 (containers, washing plate), 22 (hat); Mighty Media, Inc. (recipe photos), 10, 14, 15, 16, 17, 18, 19, 20, 21, 22, 23, 24, 25, 26, 27, 29; Shutterstock Images, 1 (rolling pin), 4 (child), 5 (all), 6 (phone, turkey, scarecrow), 8 (all), 9 (all), 10 (knife, spreader), 11 (cupcake), 14 (cornucopia cutout), 16 (pumpkin cutouts), 20 (turkey), 22 (pumpkin), 24 (drumstick cutouts), 26 (corn), 28–29 (child), 29 (plate, rolling pin), 30 (all), 31 (child)
Design Elements: Shutterstock Images (abstract doodles, kitchen utensil doodles)

Library of Congress Control Number: 2024938371

Publisher's Cataloging-in-Publication Data
Names: Anderhagen, Anna, author.
Title: Thanksgiving chuckles & chow / by Anna Anderhagen
Description: Minneapolis, Minnesota : ABDO Publishing, 2025 | Series: Holiday jokes & sweet treats | Includes online resources and index.
Identifiers: ISBN 9781098295219 (lib. bdg.) | ISBN 9798384915263 (ebook)
Subjects: LCSH: Jokes--Juvenile literature. | Thanksgiving Day--Juvenile literature. | Holidays--Juvenile literature. | Snack foods--Juvenile literature. | Cooking--Juvenile literature. | Thanksgiving cooking--Juvenile literature.
Classification: DDC 398.7--dc23

TO ADULT HELPERS

The sweet treats in this series are fun and simple. There are just a few things to remember to keep kids safe. Creating some treats requires the use of hot objects. Also, kids may be using messy materials, such as food coloring. Make sure they protect their clothes and work surfaces. Review the projects before starting and be ready to assist when necessary.

Super Sandcastle™ books are created by a team of professional educators, reading specialists, and content developers around five essential components—phonemic awareness, phonics, vocabulary, text comprehension, and fluency—to assist young readers as they develop reading skills and strategies and increase their general knowledge. All books are written, reviewed, and leveled for guided reading and early reading intervention programs for use in shared, guided, and independent reading and writing activities to support a balanced approach to literacy instruction.

Contents

THANKSGIVING

Did you know the **celebration** of Thanksgiving started long before the **Pilgrims** came to America? For thousands of years, **Indigenous** peoples in North America have celebrated the harvest with dancing and feasting. One example is the Green Corn Ceremony. After the harvest was a time for forgiveness, friendship, and being thankful.

Early European **immigrants** in North America also held thanksgiving events. They were religious services for people to pray in thanks for food or other blessings.. But these services weren't all on the same day.

In 1863, President Abraham Lincoln established the last Thursday of November as a national day of thanksgiving. Then in 1941, President Franklin D. Roosevelt signed a law that officially made the fourth Thursday in November Thanksgiving Day.

Abraham Lincoln **Franklin D. Roosevelt**

Holiday Hoots!

Can someone pick up the turkey's phone?

It's wing-ing.

Why did the turkey cross the road?

To prove it wasn't a chicken!

What do sweet potatoes wear to bed?

Yam-mies.

Why didn't the scarecrow go back for seconds at Thanksgiving dinner?

He was already stuffed.

What do you wear to Thanksgiving dinner?

A har-vest.

Why didn't the cook season the Thanksgiving turkey?

There was no thyme!

Where do turkeys go if they want to dance?

The butter-ball.

What do you call a running turkey?

Fast food.

Sweet Materials

Here are some of the ingredients and tools you will need to make the treats in this book.

Ingredients

- BelVita soft-baked breakfast biscuits
- candy corn
- candy eyes
- candy pumpkins
- chocolate almond bark
- chocolate chips
- chocolate cupcakes
- chocolate frosting
- flower-shaped ginger cookies
- fudge-covered round cookies
- glazed doughnut holes
- gold pearl sprinkles and other edible decorations
- ground cinnamon, nutmeg & cloves
- mini peanut butter cups
- mini pumpkin sprinkles
- oatmeal cream pies
- peanut-shaped peanut butter cookies
- pretzel rods & twists
- red gel icing
- Reese's Pieces candies
- Rice Krispies cereal
- vanilla frosting
- waffle cones

Tools

- baking sheet
- knife & cutting board
- large bowl
- measuring cups & spoons
- microwave-safe bowl
- oven mitts
- paper towels
- parchment paper
- serving plate
- spoons
- toothpick
- tweezers

What did Pilgrims use to bake cookies?

May-flour!

What did the salt and pepper say to welcome their Thanksgiving guests?

Season's greetings!

Frosting Tips & Tricks

Some of the recipes in this book require frosting. Here are some tips for frosting success!

Use a spatula or table knife to spread frosting

- These tools make it easy to scoop the frosting out of the jar or bowl.
- You can use them to spread the frosting smoothly or make swirls or other designs.

What kind of chocolates do you buy at the airport?

Plane ones.

Let baked items cool before frosting them

- If they are still warm, the frosting will melt.
- Cold baked items are firmer and hold their shape better while being frosted.
- To cool them faster, put them in the refrigerator.

What do cupcakes say during hide-and-seek?

Ready or not, here I crumb!

How to keep crumbs out of your frosting

- Spread a very thin coating of frosting on the baked items. Then chill them in the refrigerator for 20 minutes. The frosting will trap any **crumbs**. Then you can frost them as usual over the thin coat.

Treats Prep

Be Safe

- Ask an adult for permission to use kitchen tools and ingredients.
- Ask an adult to help you use the microwave.
- Ask an adult for help when handling sharp or hot objects.
- Clean up spills right away.

Did you hear about the scarecrow who won first prize?

It was outstanding in its field.

Get Ready!

- Wash your hands.
- Clean your work surface before you start.
- Read the list of tools and ingredients for the sweet treat you are making. Set out everything you will need.
- Read the whole recipe at least once before you start.

When You Are Finished

- Let hot treats cool completely.
- Put all the ingredients and tools away.
- Store leftover ingredients to use later.
- Wash all the dishes and cooking tools.
- Clean your work surface.
- Wash your hands before you eat your sweet treats!

Waffle Cornucopias

Why did the apple pie cry?

Its peelings were hurt!

Ingredients

- 1 box of waffle cones
- 4 2-ounce squares of chocolate almond bark
- gold pearl sprinkles and other edible decorations
- candy pumpkins, candy corn, and other fall-themed candy

Tools

- paper towels
- oven mitts
- knife & cutting board
- microwave-safe bowl
- spoon
- baking sheet
- parchment paper

TASTY!

1. Wrap a wet paper towel around the tip of a waffle cone. Microwave the cone for 20 seconds. The paper towel will get hot! Wear oven mitts when you take it out. Keep microwaving the cone 10 seconds at a time until you can gently bend the tip into a curve. You may have to rewet the paper towel. Repeat with the other cones.

2. Cut the almond bark into small **chunks**. Put them in a microwave-safe bowl. Microwave for 20 seconds at a time, stirring after each time. Repeat until the almond bark becomes creamy and smooth.

3. Line the baking sheet with parchment paper.

4. Dip the open end of a waffle cone in the melted almond bark. Place it on the baking sheet. Immediately decorate the edge with gold pearl sprinkles and other edible decorations.

5. Repeat step 4 until all of the cones have been dipped and decorated. Wait 10 minutes for the almond bark to cool.

6. Fill the cones with fall-themed candy to complete the **cornucopias**. Serve them to your friends and family for Thanksgiving!

Gourd-geous Gourds

How do you fix a broken pumpkin?
With a pumpkin patch!

WOW!

Ingredients

- red licorice ropes
- green candy strips
- 3 tablespoons butter
- 16-ounce package of mini marshmallows
- 2–5 drops orange gel food coloring
- 6 cups Rice Krispies cereal
- ½ teaspoon ground cinnamon
- ¼ teaspoon ground nutmeg
- ⅛ teaspoon ground cloves
- pretzel twists

Tools

- scissors
- ruler
- microwave-safe bowl
- cooking spray
- silicone spatula
- measuring cups and spoons
- baking sheet
- parchment paper
- plastic gloves (optional)
- chopstick

1. Cut about 30 5-inch (13 cm) pieces of licorice. Cut green candy strips into leaf and vine shapes.
2. Put the butter and marshmallows in a microwave-safe bowl. Microwave on high for 2 minutes. Add the food coloring. Grease the spatula with cooking spray and stir. Microwave for 1 minute. Stir until smooth.
3. Add the cereal, cinnamon, nutmeg, and cloves. Grease the spatula and stir until the cereal is coated.
4. Line the baking sheet with parchment paper.

5. Grease your hands, or put on gloves and grease them. Shape the mixture into balls. Set them on the baking sheet.

What is the best thing to put into pumpkin pie?

Your teeth!

Continued on the next page.

6. Break pretzel twists in half. Stick one into the top of each ball. These are the **gourds**' stems.
7. Separate the **strands** of the licorice pieces. Wrap five strands around each gourd from the stem to the bottom. Space the strands evenly. Press the licorice into the sides of the gourds. Tuck the top ends under the stem to hold them in place.
8. Place green candy leaves and vines next to the stems. Wrap the vines around a chopstick to make them curly.
9. Let the gourds cool for 10 minutes before serving.

GOURD-GEOUS!

Knock, knock!

Who's there?

Bacon.

Bacon who?

Bacon a pumpkin pie. Want some?

Turkey Gobblers

What do you get if you cross a turkey with a ghost?

A poultry-geist.

Ingredients

- 5 unfrosted chocolate cupcakes
- chocolate frosting
- 5 flower-shaped ginger cookies
- Reese's Pieces candies
- 5 glazed doughnut holes
- 10 candy eyes
- 5 pieces of candy corn
- 5 peanut-shaped peanut butter cookies

Tools

- table knife
- baking sheet
- parchment paper
- toothpick

GOBBLE!

1. Frost the tops of the cupcakes.
2. Line the baking sheet with parchment paper.
3. Frost half of each ginger cookie. Press Reese's Pieces candies into the frosting. These are the turkeys' tail feathers. Lay them on the baking sheet.
4. Cut a small slice off each doughnut hole to make a flat side. The flat sides are the bottoms of the turkeys' heads. Use a toothpick to put frosting on the backs of the candy eyes. Attach the candy eyes near the tops of the turkeys' heads.
5. Cut the big end off each piece of candy corn. Cut a slit in each head just below the eyes. Stick the cut end of a candy corn piece into each slit. These are the turkeys' beaks.
6. Set a turkey head in the middle of each cupcake.
7. Cut the peanut butter cookies in half. These are the turkeys' wings. Stick the cut ends of two wings into each cupcake on either side of the head.
8. Stick a tail into each cupcake behind the head.
9. Serve to your guests for Thanksgiving!

Pilgrim Hats

What's a Pilgrim's favorite dance?
The turkey trot.

COOL!

Ingredients

- round fudge-covered cookies
- mini peanut butter cups
- red gel icing
- candy-coated peanut butter candies
- mini pumpkin sprinkles

Tools

- baking sheet
- parchment paper
- tweezers

1. Line the baking sheet with parchment paper. Lay the fudge-covered cookies on the baking sheet.
2. Unwrap the peanut butter cups. Put red icing on the top of each one. Turn them over and place one in the center of each cookie.
3. Put a line of icing around each peanut butter cup. Press a candy-coated peanut butter candy into the icing on each cookie.
4. Use tweezers to put pumpkin sprinkles on the lines of icing.
5. Serve the Pumpkin **Pilgrim** Hats to your friends and family for Thanksgiving!

What kind of music did the Pilgrims listen to?

Plymouth Rock.

Sweet Turkey Drumsticks

What kind of key can't open doors?
A turkey.

Ingredients

- pretzel rods
- 1 box of oatmeal cream pies
- ½ cup chocolate chips

Tools

- baking sheet
- parchment paper
- large bowl
- spoons
- plastic gloves (optional)
- measuring cup
- microwave-safe bowl

YUM!

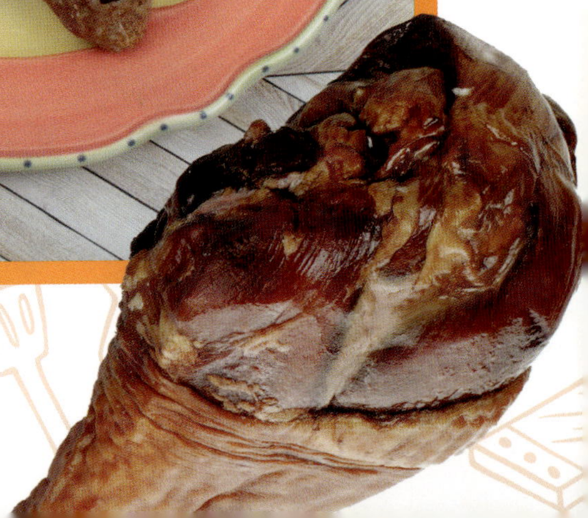

1. Break pretzel rods in half. Line the baking sheet with parchment paper.
2. Unwrap the oatmeal cream pies. Put them in a large bowl. Use a spoon or your hands to smash and mix them. You can wear plastic gloves if you like.
3. Mold a handful of oatmeal mixture around one end of each pretzel rod to form turkey drumsticks. Place them on the baking sheet.
4. Put the chocolate chips in a microwave-safe bowl. Microwave the chips for 20 seconds at a time, stirring after each time. Repeat until melted and smooth.

5. **Drizzle** the melted chocolate over the drumsticks. Put them in the refrigerator for 30 minutes before serving.

What is a chocolate's favorite day of the week?

Sundae.

Thanksgiving Corn Treats

How much does a pirate pay for corn?

A buck-an-ear!

Ingredients

- can of vanilla frosting
- BelVita soft-baked breakfast biscuits
- Reese's Pieces candies

Tools

- table knife
- serving plate

A-MAIZE-ING!

1. Spread frosting on the biscuits.
2. Arrange Reese's Pieces candies in rows on the biscuits so they look like multicolored corn.
3. Serve to your friends and family for Thanksgiving!

What did the corn say when it received a compliment?

Aw, shucks!

Keep Creating!

You've made some **delicious** treats with the recipes in this book! Hopefully you had some laughs with your friends too. But could you make any of the recipes differently? Could you use different ingredients? Or can you think of your own Thanksgiving Day treat?

Do you or a friend have a nut **allergy**? Try making the Turkey Gobbler wings with vanilla wafers instead of peanut butter cookies. For the Pumpkin **Pilgrim** Hats, you could use Rolo caramel candies instead of mini peanut butter cups. For the Thanksgiving Corn Treats, try using candy-coated chocolates instead of Reese's Pieces candies.

Does a treat include an ingredient you don't like? Get creative! Find something else to use that you do like. For example, you could use sugar cones instead of waffle cones for the **cornucopias**.

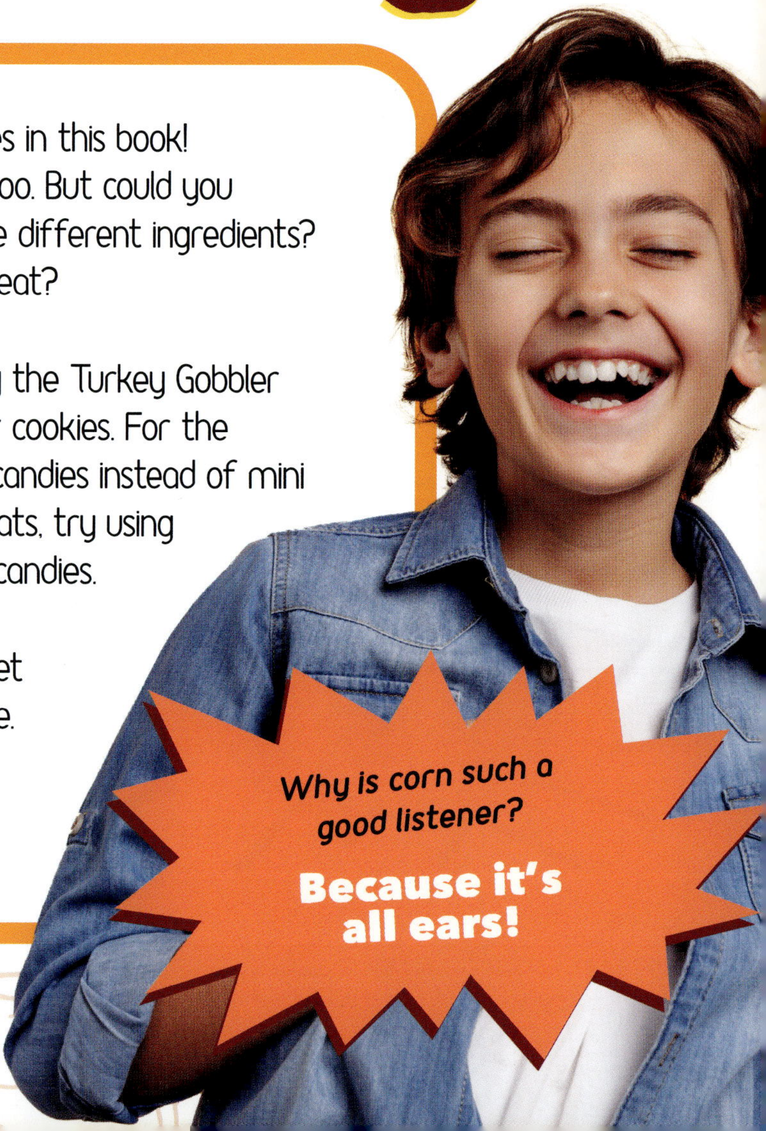

Why is corn such a good listener?

Because it's all ears!

Just use your imagination to keep creating!

Last Laughs

Why did they let the turkey join the band?

Because it had its own drumsticks.

What do you call a sad cranberry?

A blueberry.

What did the leftover turkey say?

Make me a sandwich!

What's one thing you'll have in common with a teddy bear on Thanksgiving?

You'll both be filled with stuffing.

Why shouldn't you set the turkey next to the pumpkin pie?

Because it will gobble, gobble, gobble it up!

What did the sweet potato say to the mashed potatoes?

I yam what I yam!

Why did the farmer have to separate the chicken and the turkey?

He sensed fowl play.

I tried a new pumpkin pie recipe.

I'm a real pie-oneer!

Glossary

allergy – a sickness caused by touching, breathing, or eating certain things.

celebration – a party or festival held to mark a special occasion.

chunk – a short, thick piece or lump of something.

cornucopia – a horn-shaped container overflowing with fruits, vegetables, and flowers used as a symbol of plenty.

crumb – a tiny piece of something, especially food.

delicious – very pleasing to taste.

drizzle – to pour in a thin stream.

gourd – one of several vegetables that grow on vines, such as pumpkin, cucumber, or melon.

immigrant – someone who has left his or her home and settled in a new country.

Indigenous – of or relating to ethnic groups descended from the first people known to live in a certain place.

Pilgrims – a group of people who came from England to America in the 1600s.

strand – one of the threads or strings that make up a rope or cord.